Testament of Solomon

Testament of Solomon
Translated by Frederick Cornwallis Conybeare

Cover image: *Winged Griffon on a Rocaille Bracket* (1745), Alexis Peyrotte (1699 - 1769)
Lay-out: www.burokd.nl

ISBN 978-94-92355-04-1

VAMzzz Publishing
P.O. Box 3340
1001 AC Amsterdam
The Netherlands
www.vamzzz.com
contactvamzzz@gmail.com

A First Century AD Grimoire

Testament of
SOLOMON

Translated by Frederick Cornwallis Conybeare

VAMzzz PUBLISHING

King Solomon
by Gustav Doré (1832 – 1883)

TESTAMENT of SOLOMON

Translated by F.C. Conybeare from the codex of the Paris Library, after the edition of Fleck, Wissensch. Reise, bd. ii. abth. 3.
This revised edition contains a numbering of the used zodiacal decans, in relation to the mentioned demons. These decan numbering is added for this publication and not found in the original. Strangely enough the decan rulers of 1-10 degrees Taurus and 1-10 degrees Scorpio are missing in the original manuscript, in a way as if they have been left out on purpose.

1.

Testament of Solomon, son of David, who was king in Jerusalem, and mastered and controlled all spirits of the air, on the earth, and under the earth. By means of them also he wrought all the transcendent works of the Temple. Telling also of the authorities they wield against men, and by what angels these demons are brought to naught.

Of the sage Solomon

Blessed art thou, O Lord God, who didst give Solomon such authority. Glory to thee and might unto the ages. Amen.

2.

And behold, when the Temple of the city of Jerusalem was being built, and the artificers were working thereat, Ornias the demon came among them toward sunset; and he took away half of the pay of the chief-deviser's little boy, as well as half his food. He also continued to suck the thumb of his right hand every day. And the child grew thin, although he was very much loved by the king.

3.

So King Solomon called the boy one day, and questioned him, saying: "Do I not love thee more than all the artisans who are working in the Temple of God? Do I not give thee double wages and a double supply of food? How is it that day by day and hour by hour thou growest thinner?"

4.

But the child said to the king: "I pray thee, O king. Listen to what has befallen all that thy child hath. After we are all released from our work on the Temple of God, after sunset, when I lie down to rest, one of the evil demons comes and takes away from me one half of my pay and one half of my food. Then he also takes hold of my right hand and sucks my thumb. And lo, my soul is oppressed, and so my body waxes thinner every day."

5.

Now when I Solomon heard this, I entered the Temple of God, and prayed with all my soul, night and day, that the demon might be delivered into my hands, and that I might gain authority over him. And it came about through my prayer that grace was given to me from the Lord Sabaoth by Michael his archangel. *[He brought me]* a little ring, having a seal consisting of an engraved stone, and said to me: "Take, O Solomon, king, son of David, the gift which the Lord God has sent thee, the highest Sabaoth. With it thou shalt lock up all demons of the earth, male and female; and with their help thou shalt build up

Jerusalem. *[But]* thou *[must]* wear this seal of God. And this engraving of the seal of the ring sent thee is a Pentalpha."

6.

And I Solomon was overjoyed, and praised and glorified the God of heaven and earth. And on the morrow I called the boy, and gave him the ring, and said to him: "take this, and at the hour in which the demon shall come unto thee, throw this ring at the chest of the demon, and say to him: 'In the name of God, King Solomon calls thee hither. And then do thou come running to me, without having any misgivings or fear in respect of aught thou mayest hear on the part of the demon."

7.

So the child took the ring, and went off; and behold, at the customary hour Ornias, the fierce demon, came like a burning fire to take the pay from the child. But the child according to the instructions received from the king, threw the ring at the chest of the demon, and said: "King Solomon calls thee hither." And then he went off at a run to the king. But the demon cried out aloud, saying: "Child, why hast thou done this to me? Take the ring off me, and I will render to thee the gold of the earth. Only take this off me, and forbear to lead me away to Solomon."

8.

But the child said to the demon: "As the Lord God of Israel liveth, I will not brook thee. So come hither." And the child came at a run, rejoicing, to the king, and said: "I have brought the demon, O king, as thou didst command me, O my master. And behold, he stands before the gates of the court of thy palace, crying out, and supplicating with a loud voice; offering me the silver and gold of the earth if I will only bring him unto thee."

9.

And when Solomon heard this, he rose up from his throne, and went outside into the vestibule of the court of his palace; and there he saw the demon, shuddering and trembling. And he said to him: "Who art thou?" And the demon answered: "I am called Ornias."

10.

And Solomon said to him: "Tell me, O demon, to what zodiacal sign thou art subject." And he answered: "To the Water-pourer. And those who are consumed with desire for the noble virgins upon earth … *[there appears to be a lacuna here]*, these I strangle. But in case there is no disposition to sleep, I am changed into three forms. Whenever men come to be enamoured of women, I metamorphose myself into a comely female; and I take hold of the men in their sleep, and play with them. And after a while

I again take to my wings, and hie me to the heavenly regions. I also appear as a lion, and I am commanded by all the demons. I am offspring of the archangel Uriel, the power of God."

11.

I Solomon, having heard the name of the archangel, prayed and glorified God, the Lord of heaven and earth. And I sealed the demon and set him to work at stone-cutting, so that he might cut the stones in the Temple, which, lying along the shore, had been brought by the Sea of Arabia. But he, fearful of the iron, continued and said to me: "I pray thee, King Solomon, let me go free; and I will bring you all the demons." And as he was not willing to be subject to me, I prayed the archangel Uriel to come and succour me; and I forthwith beheld the archangel Uriel coming down to me from the heavens.

12.

And the angel bade the whales of the sea come out of the abyss. And he cast his destiny upon the ground, and that [destiny] made subject [to him] the great demon. And he commanded the great demon and bold Ornias, to cut stones at the Temple. And accordingly I Solomon glorified the God of heaven and Maker of the earth. And he bade Ornias come with his destiny, and gave him the seal, saying: "Away with thee, and bring me hither the prince of all the demons."

13.

So Ornias took the finger-ring, and went off to Beelzeboul,
who has kingship over the demons. He said to him: "Hither!
Solomon calls thee." But Beelzeboul, having heard, said to him:
"Tell me, who is this Solomon of whom thou speakest to me?"
Then Ornias threw the ring at the chest of Beelzeboul, saying:
"Solomon the king calls thee." But Beelzeboul cried aloud with
a mighty voice, and shot out a great burning flame of fire;
and he arose, and followed Ornias, and came to Solomon.

14.

And when I saw the prince of demons, I glorified the Lord
God, Maker of heaven and earth, and I said: "Blessed art
thou, Lord God Almighty, who hast given to Solomon
thy servant wisdom, the assessor of the wise, and
hast subjected unto me all the power of he devil."

15.

And I questioned him, and said: "Who art thou?" The demon
replied: "I am Beelzebub, the exarch of the demons. And all the
demons have their chief seats close to me. And I it is who make
manifest the apparition of each demon." And he promised to
bring to me in bonds all the unclean spirits. And I again glorified
the God of heaven and earth, as I do always give thanks to him.

16.

I then asked of the demon if there were females among them. And when he told me that there were, I said that I desired to see them. So Beelzeboul went off at high speed, and brought unto me Onoskelis, that had a very pretty shape, and the skin of a fair-hued woman; and she tossed her head.

17.

And when she was come, I said to her: "Tell me who art thou?" But she said to me: "I am called Onoskelis, a spirit wrought ... *[?shabtai/Saturn?]*, lurking upon the earth. There is a golden cave where I lie. But I have a place that ever shifts. At one time I strangle men with a noose; at another, I creep up from the nature to the arms *[in marg: "worms"]*. But my most frequent dwelling-places are the precipices, caves, ravines. Oftentimes, however, do I consort with men in the semblance of a woman, and above all with those of a dark skin. For they share my star with me; since they it is who privily or openly worship my star, without knowing that they harm themselves, and but whet my appetite for further mischief. For they wish to provide money by means of memory (commemoration?), but I supply a little to those who worship me fairly."

18.

And I Solomon questioned her about her birth, and she replied: "I was born of a voice untimely, the so-called echo of a man's ordure dropped in a wood."

19.

And I said to her: "Under what star dost thou pass?" And she
answered me: "Under the star of the full moon, for the reason
that the moon travels over most things." Then I said to her:
"And what angel is it that frustrates thee?" And she said to
me: "He that in thee *[or "through thee"]* is reigning." And I
thought that she mocked me, and bade a soldier strike her. But
she cried aloud, and said: "I am *[subjected]* to thee, O king,
by the wisdom of God given to thee, and by the angel Joel."

20.

So I commanded her to spin the hemp for the ropes used in
the building of the house of God; and accordingly, when I
had sealed and bound her, she was so overcome and brought
to naught as to stand night and day spinning the hemp.

21.

And I at once bade another demon to be led unto me; and instantly
there approached me the demon Asmodeus, bound, and I asked
him: "Who art thou?" But he shot on me a glance of anger and
rage, and said: "And who art thou?" And I said to him: "Thus
punished as thou art, answerest thou me?" But he, with rage,
said to me: "But how shall I answer thee, for thou art a son of
man; whereas I was born an angel's seed by a daughter of man,
so that no word of our heavenly kind addressed to the earth-
born can be overweening. Wherefore also my star is bright in
heaven, and men call it, some the Wain, and some the dragon's

child. I keep near unto this star. So ask me not many things; for thy kingdom also after a little time is to be disrupted, and thy glory is but for a season. And short will be thy tyranny over us; and then we shall again have free range over mankind, so as that they shall revere us as if we were gods, not knowing, men that they are, the names of the angels set over us."

22.

And I Solomon, on hearing this, bound him more carefully, and ordered him to be flogged with thongs of ox-hide, and to tell me humbly what was his name and what his business. And he answered me thus: "I am called Asmodeus among mortals, and my business is to plot against the newly wedded, so that they may not know one another. And I sever them utterly by many calamities, and I waste away the beauty of virgin women, and estrange their hearts."

23.

And I said to him: "Is this thy only business?" And he answered me: "I transport men into fits of madness and desire, when they have wives of their own, so that they leave them, and go off by night and day to others that belong to other men; with the result that they commit sin, and fall into murderous deeds."

24.

And I adjured him by the name of the Lord Sabaôth, saying: "Fear God, Asmodeus, and tell me by what angel thou art frustrated."

But he said: "By Raphael, the archangel that stands before the throne of God. But the liver and gall of a fish put me to flight, when smoked over ashes of the tamarisk." I again asked him, and said: "Hide not aught from me. For I am Solomon, son of David, King of Israel. Tell me the name of the fish which thou reverest." And he answered: "It is the Glanos by name, and is found in the rivers of Assyria; wherefore it is that I roam about in those parts."

25.

And I said to him: "Hast thou nothing else about thee, Asmodeus?" And he answered: "The power of God knoweth, which hath bound me with the indissoluble bonds of yonder one's seal, that whatever I have told thee is true. I pray thee, King Solomon, condemn me not to [go into] water." But I smiled, and said to him: "As the Lord God of my fathers liveth, I will lay iron on thee to wear. But thou shalt also make the clay for the entire construction of the Temple, treading it down with thy feet." And I ordered them to give him ten water-jars to carry water in. And the demon groaned terribly, and did the work I ordered him to do. And this I did, because that fierce demon Asmodeus knew even the future. And I Solomon glorified God, who gave wisdom to me Solomon his servant. And the liver of the fish and its gall I hung on the spike of a reed, and burned it over Asmodeus because of his being so strong, and his unbearable malice was thus frustrated.

26.

And I summoned again to stand before me Beelzeboul, the prince of demons, and I sat him down on a raised seat of honour, and said to him: "Why art thou alone, prince of the demons?" And he said to me: "Because I alone am left of the angels of heaven that came down. For I was first angel in the first heaven being entitled Beelzeboul. And now I control all those who are bound in Tartarus. But I too have a child, and he haunts the Red Sea. And on any suitable occasion he comes up to me again, being subject to me; and reveals to me what he has done, and I support him.

27.

I Solomon said unto him: "Beelzeboul, what is thy employment?" And he answered me: "I destroy kings. I ally myself with foreign tyrants. And my own demons I set on to men, in order that the latter may believe in them and be lost. And the chosen servants of God, priests and faithful men, I excite unto desires for wicked sins, and evil heresies, and lawless deeds; and they obey me, and I bear them on to destruction. And I inspire men with envy, and *[desire for]* murder, and for wars and sodomy, and other evil things. And I will destroy the world."

28.

So I said to him: "Bring to me thy child, who is, as thou sayest, in the Red Sea." But he said to me: "I will not bring him to thee. But there shall come to me another demon called Ephippas. Him will I bind, and he will bring him up from the deep unto

me." And I said to him: "How comes thy son to be in the depth
of the sea, and what is his name? "And he answered me: "Ask
me not, for thou canst not learn from me. However, he will
come to thee by any command, and will tell thee openly."

29.

I said to him: "Tell me by what angel thou art frustrated."
And he answered: "By the holy and precious name of
the Almighty God, called by the Hebrews by a row of
numbers, of which the sum is 644, and among the Greeks
it is Emmanuel. And if one of the Romans adjure me by the
great name of the power Eleéth, I disappear at once."

30.

I Solomon was astounded when I heard this; and I ordered
him to saw up Theban1 marbles. And when he began to
saw the marbles, the other demons cried out with a loud
voice, howling because of their king Beelzeboul.

31.

But I Solomon questioned him, saying: "If thou wouldst
gain a respite, discourse to me about the things in heaven."
And Beelzeboul said: "Hear, O king, if thou burn gum, and
incense, and bulb of the seal, with nard and saffron, and
light seven lamps in an earthquake, thou wilt firmly fix thy
house. And if, being pure, thou light them at dawn in the sun
alight, then wilt thou see the heavenly dragons, how they

wind themselves along and drag the chariot of the sun."

32.
And I Solomon, having heard this, rebuked him, and said: "Silence for this present1, and continue to saw the marbles as I commanded thee." And I Solomon praised God, and commanded another demon to present himself to me. And one came before me who carried his face high up in the air, but the rest of the spirit curled away like a snail. And it broke through the few soldiers, and raised also a terrible dust on the ground, and carried it upwards; and then again hurled it back to frighten us, and asked what questions I could ask as a rule. And I stood up, and spat on the ground in that spot, and sealed with the ring of God. And forthwith the dust-wind stopped. Then I asked him, saying: "Who art thou, O wind?" Then he once more shook up a dust, and answered me: "What wouldst thou have, King Solomon?" I answered him: "Tell me what thou art called, and I would fain ask thee a question. But so far I give thanks to God who has made me wise to answer their evil plots."

33.
But *[the demon]* answered me: "I am the spirit of the ashes (Tephras)." And I said to him: "What is thy pursuit?" And he said: "I bring darkness on men, and set fire to fields; and I bring homesteads to naught. But most busy am I in summer. However, when I get an opportunity, I creep into corners of the wall, by night and day. For I am offspring of the great one, and nothing less." Accordingly I said to him: "Under what star

dost thou lie?" And he answered: "In the very tip of the moon's horn, when it is found in the south. There is my star. For I have been bidden to restrain the convulsions of the hemitertian fever; and this is why many men pray to the hemitertian fever, using these three names: Bultala, Thallal, Melchal. And I heal them." And I said to him: "I am Solomon; when therefore thou wouldst do harm, by whose aid dost thou do it?" But he said to me: "By the angel's, by whom also the third day's fever is lulled to rest." So I questioned him, and said: "And by what name?" And he answered: "That of the archangel Azael." And I summoned the archangel Azael, and set a seal on the demon, and commanded him to seize great stones, and toss them up to the workmen on the higher parts of the Temple. And, being compelled, the demon began to do what he was bidden to do.

34.

And I glorified God afresh who gave me this authority, and ordered another demon to come before me. And there came seven spirits, females, bound and woven together, fair in appearance and comely. And I Solomon, seeing them, questioned them and said: "Who are ye?" But they, with one accord, said with one voice: "We are of the thirty-three elements of the cosmic ruler of the darkness." And the first said: "I am Deception." The second said: "I am Strife." The third: "I am Klothod, which is battle." The fourth: "I am Jealousy." The fifth: "I am Power." The sixth: "I am Error." The seventh: "I am the worst of all, and our stars are in heaven. Seven stars humble in sheen, and all together. And we are called as it were goddesses. We change our place all and together, and together we live, sometimes in Lydia, sometimes in Olympus, sometimes in a great mountain."

35.
So I Solomon questioned them one by one, beginning with the first, and going down to the seventh. The first said: "I am Deception, I deceive and weave snares here and there. I whet and excite heresies. But I have an angel who frustrates me, Lamechalal."

36.
Likewise also the second said: "I am Strife, strife of strifes. I bring timbers, stones, hangers, my weapons on the spot. But I have an angel who frustrates me, Baruchiachel."

37.
Likewise also the third said: "I am called Klothod, which is Battle, and I cause the well-behaved to scatter and fall foul one of the other. And why do I say so much? I have an angel that frustrates me: "Marmarath."

38.
Likewise also the fourth said: "I cause men to forget their sobriety and moderation. I part them and split them into parties; for Strife follows me hand in hand. I rend the husband from the sharer of his bed, and children from parents, and

brothers from sisters. But why tell so much to my despite?
I have an angel that frustrates me, the great Balthial."

39.

Likewise also the fifth said: "I am Power. By power I raise
up tyrants and tear down kings. To all rebels I furnish
power. I have an angel that frustrates me, Asteraôth."

40.

Likewise also the sixth said: "I am Error, O King Solomon. And
I will make thee to err, as I have before made thee to err, when
I caused thee to slay thy own brother. I will lead you into error,
so as to pry into graves; and I teach them that dig, and I lead
errant souls away from all piety, and many other evil traits
are mine. But I have an angel that frustrates me, Uriel."

41.

Likewise also the seventh said: "I am the worst, and I make
thee worse off than thou wast; because I will impose the bonds
of Artemis. But the locustI will set me free, for by means
thereof is it fated that thou shalt achieve my desire ...... For
if one were wise, he would not turn his steps toward me."

42.

So I Solomon, having heard and wondered, sealed them with my
ring; and since they were so considerable, I bade them dig the
foundations of the Temple of God. For the length of it was 250

cubits. And I bade them be industrious, and with one murmur
of joint protest they began to perform the tasks enjoined.

43.

But I Solomon glorified the Lord, and bade another demon
come before me. And there was brought to me a demon
having all the limbs of a man, but without a head. And I,
seeing him, said to him: "Tell me, who art thou?" And he
answered: "I am a demon." So I said to him: "Which?" And he
answered me: "I am called Envy. For I delight to devour heads,
being desirous to secure for myself a head; but I do not eat
enough, but am anxious to have such a head as thou hast."

44.

I Solomon, on hearing this, sealed him, stretching out my hand
against his chest. Whereon the demon leapt up, and threw himself
down, and gave a groan, saying: "Woe is me! where am I come to?
O traitor Ornias, I cannot see!" So I said to him: "I am Solomon.
Tell me then how thou dost manage to see." And he answered
me: "By means of my feelings." I then, Solomon, having heard his
voice come up to me, asked him how he managed to speak. And
he answered me: "I, O King Solomon, am wholly voice, for I have
inherited the voices of many men. For in the case of all men who
are called dumb, I it is who smashed their heads, when they were
children and had reached their eighth day. Then when a child is
crying in the night, I become a spirit, and glide by means of his
voice. . . . In the crossways1 also I have many services to render,

and my encounter is fraught with harm. For I grasp in all instant a man's head, and with my hands, as with a sword, I cut it off, and put it on to myself. And in this way, by means of the fire which is in me, through my neck it is swallowed up. I it is that sends grave mutilations and incurable on men's feet, and inflict sores."

45.

And I Solomon, on hearing this, said to him: "Tell me how thou dost discharge forth the fire? Out of what sources dost thou emit it?" And the spirit said to me: "From the Day-star1. For here hath not yet been found that Elburion, to whom men offer prayers and kindle lights. And his name is invoked by the seven demons before me. And he cherishes them."

46.

But I said to him: "Tell me his name." But he answered: "I cannot tell thee. For if I tell his name, I render myself incurable. But he will come in response to his name." And on hearing this, I Solomon said to him: "Tell me then, by what angel thou art frustrated?" And he answered: "By the fiery flash of lightning." And I bowed myself before the Lord God of Israel, and bade him remain in the keeping of Beelzeboul until lax should come.

47.

Then I ordered another demon to come before me, and there came into my presence a hound, having a very large shape, and it spoke with a loud voice, and said, "Hail, Lord, King Solomon!"

And I Solomon was astounded. I said to it: Who art thou, O hound?" And it answered: "I do indeed seem to thee to be a hound, but before thou wast, O King Solomon, I was a man that wrought many unholy deeds on earth. I was surpassingly learned in letters, and was so mighty that I could hold the stars of heaven back. And many divine works did I prepare. For I do harm to men who follow after our star, and turn them to . . . . And I seize the frenzied men by the larynx, and so destroy them."

48.

And I Solomon said to him: "What is thy name?" And he answered: "Staff" (Rabdos). And I said to him: "What is thine employment? And what results canst thou achieve?" And he replied: "Give me thy man, and I will lead him away into a mountainous spot, and will show him a green stone tossed to and fro, with which thou mayest adorn the temple of the Lord God."

49.

And I Solomon, on hearing this, ordered my servant to set off with him, and to take the finger-ring bearing the seal of God with him. And I said to him: "Whoever shall show thee the green stone, seal him with this finger-ring. And mark the spot with care, and bring me the demon hither. And the demon showed him the green stone, and he sealed it, and brought the demon to me. And I Solomon decided to confine with my seal on my right hand the two, the headless demon, likewise the hound, that was so huge1; he should be bound as well. And I bade the hound keep safe the fiery spirit so that lamps as it were might by day and night cast their light through its maw on the artisans at work.

50.
And I Solomon took from the mine of that stone 200 shekels for the supports of the table of incense, which was similar in appearance. And I Solomon glorified the Lord God, and then closed round the treasure of that stone. And I ordered afresh the demons to cut marble for the construction of the house of God. And I Solomon prayed to the Lord, and asked the hound, saying: "By what angel art thou frustrated?" And the demon replied: "By the great Brieus."

51.
And I praised the Lord God of heaven and earth, and bade another demon come forward to me; and there came before me one in the form of a lion roaring. And he stood and answered me saying: "O king, in the form which I have, I am a spirit quite incapable of being perceived. Upon all men who lie prostrate with sickness I leap, coming stealthily along; and I render the man weak, so that his habit of body is enfeebled. But I have also another glory, O king. I cast out demons, and I have legions under my control. And I am capable of being received1 in my dwelling-places, along with all the demons belonging to the legions under me." But I Solomon, on hearing this, asked him: "What is thy name?" But he answered: "Lion-bearer, Rath in kind." And I said to him: "How art thou to be frustrated along with thy legions? What angel is it

that frustrates thee?" And he answered: "If I tell thee my name, I bind not myself alone, but also the legions of demons under me."

52.

So I said to him: "I adjure thee in the name of the God Sabaoth, to tell me by what name thou art frustrated along with thy host." And the spirit answered me: "The 'great among men,' who is to suffer many things at the hands of men, whose name is the figure 644, which is Emmanuel; he it is who has bound us, and who will then come and plunge us from the steep under water. He is noised abroad in the three letters which bring him down."

53.

And I Solomon, on hearing this, glorified God, and condemned his legion to carry wood from the thicket. And I condemned the lion-shaped one himself to saw up the wood small with his teeth, for burning in the unquenchable furnace for the Temple of God.

54.

And I worshipped the Lord God of Israel, and bade another demon come forward. And there came before me a dragon, three-headed, of fearful hue. And I questioned him: "Who art thou?" And he answered me: "I am a caltrop-like spirit1, whose activity in three lines. But I blind children in women's wombs, and twirl their ears round. And I make them deaf and mute. And I have again in my third head means of slipping in. And I smite men in the limbless part of the body, and cause them to fall down, and foam, and grind their teeth. But I have my own way of being frustrated, Jerusalem being signified in writing, unto the place called 'of the head4." For there is fore-appointed the angel of the great counsel, and now he will openly dwell on the cross. He doth frustrate me, and to him am I subject."

55.

"But in the place where thou sittest, O King Solomon, standeth a column in the air, of purple...1 The demon called Ephippas hath brought [it] up from the Red Sea, from inner Arabia. He it is that shall be shut up in a skin-bottle and brought before thee. But at the entrance of the Temple, which thou hast begun to build, O King Solomon, lies stored much gold, which dig thou up and carry off." And I Solomon sent my servant, and found it to be as the demon told me. And I sealed him with my ring, and praised the Lord God."

56.

So I said to him: "What art thou called?" And the demon said: "I am the crest of dragons." And I bade him make bricks in the Temple. He had human hands.

57.

And I adored the Lord God of Israel, and bade another demon present himself. And there came before me a spirit in woman's form, that had a head without any limbs1, and her hair was dishevelled. And I said to her: "Who art thou?" But she answered: "Nay, who art thou? And why dost thou want to hear concerning me? But, as thou wouldst learn, here l stand bound before thy face. Go then into thy royal storehouses and wash thy hands. Then sit down afresh before thy tribunal, and ask me questions; and thou shalt learn, O king, who l am."

58.

And l Solomon did as she enjoined me, and restrained myself because of the wisdom dwelling in me1; in order that l might hear of her deeds, and reprehend them, and manifest them to men. And l sat down, and said to the demon: "What art thou?" And she said: "l am called among men Obizuth; and by night l sleep not, but go my rounds over all the world, and visit women in childbirth. And divining the hour l take my stand; and if l am lucky, l strangle the child. But if not, l retire to another place. For l cannot for a single night retire unsuccessful. For l am a fierce spirit, of myriad names and many shapes. And now hither, now thither l roam. And to westering parts l go my rounds. But as it now is, though thou hast sealed me round with the ring of God, thou hast done nothing. l am not standing before thee, and thou wilt not be able to command me. For l have no work other than the destruction of children, and the making their ears to be deaf, and the working of evil to their eyes, and the binding their mouths with a bond, and the ruin of their minds, and paining of their bodies."

59.

When I Solomon heard this, I marvelled at her appearance,
for I beheld all her body to be in darkness. But her glance was
altogether bright and greeny, and her hair was tossed wildly
like a dragon's; and the whole of her limbs were invisible. And
her voice was very clear as it came to me. And I cunningly said:
"Tell me by what angel thou art frustrated, O evil spirit?" By
she answered me: "By the angel of God called Afarôt, which
is interpreted Raphael, by whom I am frustrated now and for
all time. His name, if any man know it, and write the same on
a woman in childbirth, then I shall not be able to enter her. Of
this name the number is 640." And I Solomon having heard this,
and having glorified the Lord, ordered her hair to be bound,
and that she should be hung up in front of the Temple of God;
that all the children of Israel, as they passed, might see it, and
glorify the Lord God of Israel, who had given me this authority,
with wisdom and power from God, by means of this signet.

60.

And I again ordered another demon to come before me.
And the came, rolling itself along, one in appearance
like to a dragon, but having the face and hands of a man.
And all its limbs, except the feet, were those of a dragon;
and it had wings on its back. And when I beheld it, I was
astonished, and said: "Who art thou, demon, and what art
thou called? And whence hast thou come? Tell me."

61.

And the spirit answered and said: "This is the first time I have stood before the, O King Solomon. I am a spirit made into a god among men, but now brought to naught by the ring and wisdom vouchsafed to thee by God. Now I am the so-called winged dragon, and I chamber not with many women, but only with a few that are of fair shape, which possess the name of xuli, of this star. And I pair with them in the guise of a spirit winged in form, coitum habens per nates. And she on whom I have leapt goes heavy with child, and that which is born of her becomes eros. But since such offspring cannot be carried by men, the woman in question breaks wind. Such is my role. Supposed then only that I am satisfied, and all the other demons molested and disturbed by thee will speak the whole truth. But those composed of fire will cause to be burned up by fire the material of the logs which is to be collected by them for the building in the Temple."

62.

And as the demon said this, I saw the spirit going forth from his mouth, and it consumed the wood of the frankincense-tree, and burned up all the logs which we had placed in the Temple of God. And I Solomon saw what the spirit had done, and I marvelled.

63.

And, having glorified God, I asked the dragon-shaped demon, and said: "Tell me, by what angel art thou frustrated?" And he answered: "By the great angel which has its seat in the second heaven, which is called in Hebrew Bazazeth. And I Solomon, having heard this, and having invoked his angel, condemned him to saw up marbles for the building of the Temple of God; and I praised God, and commanded another demon to come before me.

64.

And there came before my face another spirit, as it were a woman in the form she had. But on her shoulders she had two other heads with hands. And I asked her, and said: "Tell me, who art thou?" And she said to me: "I am Enêpsigos, who also have a myriad names." And I said her: "By what angel art thou frustrated?" But she said to me: "What seekest, what askest thou? I undergo changes, like the goddess I am called. And I change again, and pass into possession of another shape. And be not desirous therefore to know all that concerns me. But since thou art before me for this much, hearken. I have my abode in the moon, and for that reason I possess three forms. At times I am magically invoked by the wise as Kronos. At other times, in connexion with those who bring me down, I come down and appear in another shape. The measure of the element is inexplicable and indefinable, and not to be frustrated. I then, changing into these three forms, come down and become such as thou seest me; but I am frustrated by the angel Rathanael, who sits in the third heaven. This then is why I speak to thee. Yonder temple cannot contain me."

65.

I therefore Solomon prayed to my God, and I invoked the angel of whom Enépsigos spoke to me, and used my seal. And I sealed her with a triple chain, and (placed) beneath her the fastening of the chain. I used the seal of God, and the spirit prophesied to me, saying: "This is what thou, King Solomon, doest to us. But after a time thy kingdom shall be broken, and again in season this Temple shall be riven asunder; and all Jerusalem shall be undone by the King of the Persians and Medes and Chaldaeans. And the vessels of this Temple, which thou makest, shall be put to servile uses of the gods; and along with them all the jars, in which thou dost shut us up, shall be broken by the hands of men. And then we shall go forth in great power hither and thither, and be disseminated all over the world. And we shall lead astray the inhabited world for a long season, until the Son of God is stretched upon the cross. For never before doth arise a king like unto him, one frustrating us all, whose mother shall not have contact with man. Who else can receive such authority over spirits, except he, whom the first devil will seek to tempt, but will not prevail over? The number of his name is 644, which is Emmanuel. Wherefore, O King Solomon, thy time is evil, and thy years short and evil, and to thy servant shall thy kingdom be given."

66.

And I Solomon, having heard this, glorified God. And though I marvelled at the apology of the demons, I did not credit it until it came true. And I did not believe their words; but when they were realized, then I understood, and at my death I wrote this Testament to the children of Israel, and gave it to them, so that they might know the powers of the demons and their shapes, and the names of their angels, by which these angels are frustrated. And I glorified the Lord God of Israel, and commanded the spirits to be bound with bonds indissoluble.

67.

And having praised God, I commanded another spirit to come before me; and there came before my face another demon, having in front the shape of a horse, but behind of a fish. And he had a mighty voice, and said to me: "O King Solomon, I am a fierce spirit of the sea, and I am greedy of gold and silver. I am such a spirit as rounds itself and comes over the expanses of the water of the sea, and I trip up the men who sail thereon. For I round myself into a wave, and transform myself, and then throw myself on ships and come right in on them. And that is my business, and my way of getting hold of money and men. For I take the men, and whirl them round with myself, and hurl the men out of the sea. For I am not covetous of men's bodies, but cast them up out of the sea so far. But since Beelzeboul, ruler of the spirits of air and of those under the earth, and lord of earthly ones, hath a joint kingship with us in respect of the deeds of each one of us, therefore I went up from the sea, to get a certain outlook in his company.

68.

"But I also have another character and role. I metamorphose myself into waves, and come up from the sea. And I show myself to men, so that those on earth call me Kuno[s]paston, because I assume the human form. And my name is a true one. For by my passage up into men, I send forth a certain nausea. I came then to take counsel with the prince Beelzeboul; and he bound me and delivered me into thy hands. And I am here before thee because of this seal, and thou dost now torment me. Behold now, in two or three days the spirit that converseth with thee will fail, because I shall have no water."

69.

And I said to him: "Tell me by what angel thou art frustrated." And he answered: "By Iameth." And I glorified God. I commanded the spirit to be thrown into a phial along with ten jugs of sea-water of two measures each. And I sealed them round above the marbles and asphalt and pitch in the mouth of the vessel. And having sealed it with my ring, I ordered it to be deposited in the Temple of God. And I ordered another spirit to come before me.

70.

And there came before my face another enslaved spirit, having obscurely the form of a man, with gleaming eyes, and bearing in his hand a blade. And I asked: "Who art thou? But he answered: "I am a lascivious spirit, engendered of a giant man who dies in the massacre in the time of the

giants." I said to him: "Tell me what thou art employed
on upon earth, and where thou hast thy dwelling."

71.

And he said: "My dwelling is in fruitful places, but my procedure
is this. I seat myself beside the men who pass along among the
tombs, and in untimely season I assume the form of the dead; and
if I catch any one, I at once destroy him with my sword. But if I
cannot destroy him, I cause him to be possessed with a demon,
and to devour his own flesh, and the hair to fall off his chin." But I
said to him: "Do thou then be in fear of the God of heaven and of
earth, and tell me by angel thou art frustrated." And he answered:
"He destroys me who is to become Saviour, a man whose number,
if any one shall write it on his forehead1, he will defeat me, and
in fear I shall quickly retreat. And, indeed, if any one write this
sign on him, I shall be in fear." And I Solomon, on hearing this, and
having glorified the Lord God, shut up this demon like the rest.

72.

And I commanded another demon to come before me. And there
came before my face thirty-six spirits, their heads shapeless like
dogs, but in themselves they were human in form; with faces of
asses, faces of oxen, and faces of birds. And I Solomon, on hearing
and seeing them, wondered, and I asked them and said: "Who
are you?" But they, of one accord with one voice, said: "We are
the thirty-six elements, the world-rulers of this darkness. But, O
King Solomon, thou wilt not wrong us nor imprison us, nor lay

command on us; but since the Lord God has given thee authority over every spirit, in the air, and on the earth, and under the earth, therefore do we also present ourselves before thee like the other spirits, from ram and bull, from both twin and crab, lion and virgin, scales and scorpion, archer, goat-horned, water-pourer, and fish.

73.

Then I Solomon invoked the name of the Lord Sabaoth, and questioned each in turn as to what was its character. And I bade each one come forward and tell of its actions. Then the first one came forward, and said: "I am the first decans of the zodiacal circle, and I am called the ram, and with me are these two." So I put to them the question: "Who are ye called?" The first said: "I, O Lord, am called Ruax, and I cause the heads of men to be idle, and I pillage their brows. But let me only hear the words, 'Michael, imprison Ruax,' and at once I retreat."
[I – ARIES]

74.

And the second said: "I am called Barsafael, and I cause those who are subject to my hour to feel the pain of migraine. If only I hear the words, 'Gabriel, imprison Barsafael,' at once I retreat."
[II - ARIES]

75.

The third said: "I am called Arôtosael. I do harm to eyes, and grievously injure them. Only let me hear the words,

'Uriel, imprison Aratosael' (sic), at once I retreat . . . . ."
[III- ARIES]

[ruler of the first decan of Taurus is missing in the manuscript]

76.
The fifth said: "I am called Iudal, and I bring about
a block in the ears and deafness of hearing. If
I hear, 'Uruel Iudal,' I at once retreat."
[II - TAURUS]

77.
The sixth said: "I am called Sphendonaêl. I cause
tumours of the parotid gland, and inflammations of
the tonsils, and tetanic recurvation. If I hear, 'Sabrael,
imprison Sphendonaêl,' at once I retreat."
[III - TAURUS]

78.
And the Seventh said: "I am called Sphandôr, and I weaken the
strength of the shoulders, and cause them to tremble; and I
paralyze the nerves of the hands, and I break and bruise the
bones of the neck. And I, I suck out the marrow. But if I hear
the words, 'Araêl, imprison Sphandôr,' I at once retreat."
[I - GEMINI]

79.

And the eight said: "l am called Belbel. l distort
the hearts and minds of men. If l hear the words,
'Araêl, imprison Belbel,' l at once retreat."
[ll - GEMINI]

80.

And the ninth said: "l am called Kurtaêl. l send colics
in the bowels. l induce pains. If l hear the words,
'Iaôth, imprison Kurtaêl,' l at once retreat."
[lll - GEMINI]

81.

The tenth said: "l am called Metathiax. l cause the reins to ache. If
l hear the words, 'Adônaêl, imprison Metathiax,' l at once retreat."
[I- CANCER]

82.

The eleventh said: "l am called Katanikotaêl. l create strife
and wrongs in men's homes, and send on them hard temper.
If any one would be at peace in his home, let him write on
seven leaves of laurel the name of the angel that frustrates me,
along with these names: Iae, Ieô, sons of Sabaôth, in the name
of the great God let him shut up Katanikotaêl. Then let him
wash the laurel-leaves in water, and sprinkle his house with
the water, from within to the outside. And at once l retreat."
[ll - CANCER]

83.

The twelfth said: "I am called Saphathoraél, and I inspire partisanship in men, and delight in causing them to stumble. If any one will write on paper these names of angels, Iacô, Iealô, Iôelet, Sabaôth, Ithoth, Bae, and having folded it up, wear it round his neck or against his ear, I at once retreat and dissipate the drunken fit."
[III - CANCER]

84.

The thirteenth said: "I am called Bobêl (sic), and I cause nervous illness by my assaults. If I hear the name of the great 'Adonaêl, imprison Bothothêl,' I at once retreat."
[I - LEO]

85.

The fourteenth said: "I am called Kumeatêl, and I inflict shivering fits and torpor. If only I hear the words: 'Zôrôêl, imprison Kumentaêl,' I at once retreat."
[II - LEO]

86.

The fifteenth said: "I am called Roêlêd. I cause cold and frost and pain in the stomach. Let me only hear the words: 'Iax, bide not, be not warmed, for Solomon is fairer than eleven fathers,' I at [once] retreat."
[III - LEO]

87.

The sixteenth said: "I am called Atrax. I inflict upon men fevers, irremediable and harmful. If you would imprison me, chop up coriander and smear it on the lips, reciting the following charm: 'The fever which is from dirt. I exorcise thee by the throne of the most high God, retreat from dirt and retreat from the creature fashioned by God.' And at once I retreat."
[I - VIRGO]

88.

The seventeenth said: "I am called Ieropaêl. On the stomach of men I sit, and cause convulsions in the bath and in the road; and wherever I be found, or find a man, I throw him down. But if any one will say to the afflicted into their ear these names, three times over, into the right ear: 'Iudarizê, Sabunê, Denôê,' I at once retreat."
[II - VIRGO]

89.

The eighteenth said: "I am called Buldumêch. I separate wife from husband and bring about a grudge between them. If any one write down the names of thy sires, Solomon, on paper and place it in the ante-chamber of his house, I retreat thence. And the legend written shall be as follows: 'The God of Abram, and the God of Isaac, and the God of Jacob commands thee -- retire from this house in peace.' And I at once retire."
[III - VIRGO]

90.

The nineteenth said: "I am called Naôth, and I take my seat on the knees of men. If any one write on paper: 'Phnunoboêol, depart Nathath, and touch thou not the neck,' I at once retreat."
[I - LIBRA]

91.

The twentieth said: "I am called Marderô. I send on men incurable fever. If any one write on the leaf of a book: 'Sphênêr, Rafael, retire, drag me not about, flay me not,' and tie it round his neck, I at once retreat."
[II - LIBRA]

92.

The twenty-first said: "I am called Alath, and I cause coughing and hard-breathing in children. If any one write on paper: 'Rorêx, do thou pursue Alath,' and fasten it round his neck, I at once retire..."
[III - LIBRA]

[ruler of the first decan of Scorpio is missing in the manuscript]

93.

The twenty-third said: "I am called Nefthada. I cause the reins to ache, and I bring about dysury. If any one write on a plate of tin the words: 'Iathôth, Uruêl, Nephthada,' and fasten it round the loins, I at once retreat."
[II - SCORPIO]

94.

The twenty-fourth said: "I am called Akton. I cause ribs and lumbic muscles to ache. If one engrave on copper material, taken from a ship which has missed its anchorage, this: 'Marmaraôth, Sabaôth, pursue Akton,' and fasten it round the loin, I at once retreat."
[III - SCORPIO]

95.

The twenty-fifth said: "I am called Anatreth, and I rend burnings and fevers into the entrails. But if I hear: 'Arara, Charara,' instantly do I retreat."
[I - SAGITTARIUS]

96.

The twenty-sixth said: "I am called Enenuth. I steal away men's minds, and change their hearts, and make a man toothless (?). If one write: 'Allazoôl, pursue Enenuth,' and tie the paper round him, I at once retreat."
[II - SAGITTARIUS]

97.

The twenty-seventh said: "I am called Phêth. I make men consumptive and cause hemorrhagia. If one exorcise me in wine, sweet-smelling and unmixed by the eleventh aeonI, and say: 'I exorcise thee by the eleventh aeon to stop, I demand, Phêth (Axiôphêth),' then give it to the patient to drink, and I at once retreat."

98.

The twenty-eighth said: "I am called Harpax, and I send sleeplessness on men. If one write 'Kokphnêdismos,' and bind it round the temples, I at once retire."
[I - CAPRICORN]

99.

The twenty-ninth said: "I am called Anostêr. I engender uterine mania and pains in the bladder. If one powder into pure oil three seeds of laurel and smear it on, saying: 'I exorcise thee, Anostêr. Stop by Marmaraô,' at once I retreat."
[II – CAPRICORN]

100.

The thirtieth said: "I am called Alleborith. If in eating fish one has swallowed a bone, then he must take a bone from the fish and cough, and at once I retreat."
[III - CAPRICORN]

101.

The thirty-first said: "I am called Hephesimireth, and cause lingering disease. If you throw salt, rubbed in the hand, into oil and smear it on the patient, saying: 'Seraphim, Cherubim, help me!' I at once retire."
[I - AQUARIUS]

102.

The thirty-second said: "I am called Ichthion. I paralyze muscles and contuse them. If I hear 'Adonaêth, help!' I at once retire."
[II - AQUARIUS]

103.

The thirty-third said: "I am called Agchoniôn. I lie among swaddling-clothes and in the precipice. And if any one write on fig-leaves 'Lycurgos,' taking away one letter at a time, and write it, reversing the letters, I retire at once. 'Lycurgos, ycurgos, kurgos, yrgos, gos, os.'"
[III - AQUARIUS]

104.

The thirty-fourth said: "I am called Autothith. I cause grudges and fighting. Therefore I am frustrated by Alpha and Omega, if written down."
[I - PISCES]

105.

The thirty-fifth said: "I am called Phthenoth. I cast evil eye on every man. Therefore, the eye much-suffering, if it be drawn. frustrates me."
[II - PISCES]

106.

The thirty-sixth said: "I am called Bianakith. I have a grudge

against the body. I lay waste houses, I cause flesh to decay, and all else that is similar. If a man write on the front-door of his house: 'Mêltô, Ardu, Anaath,' I flee from that place."
[III- PISCES]

107.
And I Solomon, when I heard this, glorified the God of heaven and earth. And I commanded them to fetch water in the Temple of God. And I furthermore prayed to the Lord God to cause the demons without, that hamper humanity, to be bound and made to approach the Temple of God. Some of these demons I condemned to do the heavy work of the construction of the Temple of God. Others I shut up in prisons. Others I ordered to wrestle with fire in (the making of) gold and silver, sitting down by lead and spoon. And to make ready places for the other demons in which they should be confined.

108.
And I Solomon had much quiet in all the earth, and spent my life in profound peace, honoured by all men and by all under heaven. And I built the entire Temple of the Lord God. And my kingdom was prosperous, and my army was with me. And for the rest the city of Jerusalem had repose, rejoicing and delighted. And all the kings of the earth came to me from the ends of the earth to behold the Temple which I builded to the Lord God. And having heard of the wisdom given to me, they did homage to me in the Temple, bringing gold and silver and precious stones, many and divers,

and bronze, and iron, and lead, and cedar logs. And woods decay
not they brought me, for the equipment of the Temple of God.

109.

And among them also the queen of the South, being a witch,
came in great concern and bowed low before me to the
earth. And having heard my wisdom, she glorified the God
of Israel, and she made formal trial of all my wisdom, of
all love in which I instructed her, according to the wisdom
imparted to me. And all the sons of Israel glorified God.

110.

And behold, in those days one of the workmen, of ripe old
age, threw himself down before me, and said: "King Solomon,
pity me, because I am old." So I bade him stand up, and said:
"Tell me, old man, all you will." And he answered: "I beseech
you king, I have an only-born son, and he insults and beats me
openly, and plucks out the hair of my head, and threatens me
with a painful death. Therefore I beseech you avenge me.

111.

And I Solomon, on hearing this, felt compunction as I looked at
his old age; and I bade the child be brought to me. And when
he was brought I questioned him whether it were true. And the
youth said: "I was not so filled with madness as to strike my
father with my hand. Be kind to me, O king. For I have not dared
to commit such impiety, poor wretch that I am." But I Solomon

on hearing this from the youth, exhorted the old man to reflect on the matter, and accept his son's apology. However, he would not, but said he would rather let him die. And as the old man would not yield, I was about to pronounce sentence on the youth, when I saw Ornias the demon laughing. I was very angry at the demon's laughing in my presence; and I ordered my men to remove the other parties, and bring forward Ornias before my tribunal. And when he was brought before me, I said to him: "Accursed one, why didst thou look at me and laugh?" And the demon answered: "Prithee, king, it was not because of thee I laughed, but because of this ill-starred old man and the wretched youth, his son. For after three days his son will die untimely; and lo, the old man desires to foully make away with him."

112.

But I Solomon, having heard this, said to the demon: "Is that true that thou speakest?" And he answered: "It is true; O king." And I, on hearing that, bade them remove the demon, and that they should again bring before me the old man with his son. I bade them make friends with one another again, and I supplied them with food. And then I told the old man after three days to bring his son again to me here; "and," said I, "I will attend to him." And they saluted me, and went their way.

113.

And when they were gone I ordered Ornias to be brought forward, and said to him: "Tell me how you know this;" and he answered: "We demons ascend into the firmament of heaven, and fly about among the stars. And we hear the sentences which go forth upon the souls of men, and forthwith we come, and whether by force of influence, or by fire, or by sword, or by some accident, we veil our act of destruction; and if a man does not die by some untimely disaster or by violence, then we demons transform ourselves in such a way as to appear to men and be worshipped in our human nature."

114.

I therefore, having heard this, glorified the Lord God, and again I questioned the demon, saying: "Tell me how ye can ascend into heaven, being demons, and amidst the stars and holy angels intermingle." And he answered: "Just as things are fulfilled in heaven, so also on earth (are fulfilled) the types of all of them. For there are principalities, authorities, world-rulers, and we demons fly about in the air; and we hear the voices of the heavenly beings, and survey all the powers. And as having no ground (basis) on which to alight and rest, we lose strength and fall off like leaves from trees. And men seeing us imagine that the stars are falling from heaven. But it is not really so, O king; but we fall because of our weakness, and because we have nowhere anything to lay hold of; and so we fall down like lightnings in the depth of night and suddenly. And we set cities in flames and fire the fields. For the stars have firm foundations in the heavens like the sun and the moon."

115.

And I Solomon, having heard this, ordered the demon to be guarded for five days. And after the five days I recalled the old man, and was about to question him. But he came to me in grief and with black face. And I said to him: "Tell me, old man, where is thy son? And what means this garb?" And he answered: "Lo, I am become childless, and sit by my son's grave in despair. For it is already two days that he is dead." But I Solomon, on hearing that, and knowing that the demon Ornias had told me the truth, glorified the God of Israel.

116.

And the queen of the South saw all this, and marvelled, glorifying the God of Israel; and she beheld the Temple of the Lord being builded. And she gave a siklos of gold and one hundred myriads of silver and choice bronze, and she went into the Temple. And (she beheld) the altar of incense and the brazen supports of this altar, and the gems of the lamps flashing forth of different colours, and of the lamp-stand of stone, and of emerald, and hyacinth, and sapphire; and she beheld the vessels of gold, and silver, and bronze, and wood, and the folds of skins dyed red with madder. And she saw the bases of the pillars of the Temple of the Lord. All were of one gold ... apart from the demons whom I condemned to labour. And there was peace in the circle of my kingdom and over all the earth.

117.

And it came to pass, which I was in my kingdom, the
King of the Arabians, Adares, sent me a letter, and the
writing of the letter was written as follows: --
"To King Solomon, all hail! Lo, we have heard, and it hath been
heard unto all the ends of the earth, concerning the wisdom
vouchsafed in thee, and that thou art a man merciful from
the Lord. And understanding hath been granted thee over all
the spirits of the air, and on earth, and under the earth. Now,
forasmuch as there is present in the land of Arabia a spirit of
the following kind: at early dawn there begins to blow a certain
wind until the third hour. And its blast is harsh and terrible,
and it slays man and beast. And no spirit can live upon earth
against this demon. I pray thee then, forasmuch as the spirit
is a wind, contrive something according to the wisdom given
in thee by the Lord thy God, and deign to send a man able to
capture it. And behold, King Solomon, I and my people and all
my land will serve thee unto death. And all Arabia shall be at
peace with thee, if thou wilt perform this act of righteousness
for us. Wherefore we pray thee, contemn not our humble prayer,
and suffer not to be utterly brought to naught the eparchy
subordinated to thy authority. Because we are suppliants, both I
and my people and all my land. Farewell to my Lord. All health!"

118.

And I Solomon read this epistle; and I folded it up and gave it
to my people, and said to them: "After seven days shalt thou

remind me of this epistle. And Jerusalem was built, and the Temple was being completed. And there was a stone1, the end stone of the corner lying there, great, chosen out, one which I desired lay in the head of the corner of the completion of the Temple. And all the workmen, and all the demons helping them came to the same place to bring up the stone and lay it on the pinnacle of the holy Temple, and were not strong enough to stir it, and lay it upon the corner allotted to it. For that stone was exceedingly great and useful for the corner of the Temple."

119.

And after seven days, being reminded of the epistle of Adares, King of Arabia, I called my servant and said to him: "Order thy camel and take for thyself a leather flask, and take also this seal. And go away into Arabia to the place in which the evil spirit blows; and there take the flask, and the signet-ring in front of the mouth of the flask, and (hold them) towards the blast of the spirit. And when the flask is blown out, thou wilt understand that the demon is (in it). Then hastily tie up the mouth of to flask, and seal it securely with the seal-ring, and lay it carefully on the camel and bring it me hither. And if on the way it offer thee gold or silver or treasure in return for letting it go, see that thou be not persuaded. But arrange without using oath to release it. And then if it point out to the places where are gold or silver, mark the places and seal them with this seal. And bring the demon to me. And now depart, and fare thee well."

120.

Then the youth did as was bidden him. And he ordered his camel, and laid on it a flask, and set off into Arabia. And the men of that region would not believe that he would be able to catch the evil spirit. And when it was dawn, the servant stood before the spirit's blast, and laid the flask on the ground, and the finger-ring on the mouth of the flask. And the demon blew through the middle of the finger-ring into the mouth of the flask, and going in blew out the flask. But the man promptly stood up to it and drew tight with his hand the mouth of the flask, in the name of the Lord God of Sabaôth. And the demon remained within the flask. And after that the youth remained in that land three days to make trial. And the spirit no longer blew against that city. And all the Arabs knew that he had safely shut in the spirit.

121.

Then the youth fastened the flask on the camel, and the Arabs sent him forth on his way with much honour and precious gifts, praising and magnifying the God of Israel. But the youth brought in the bag and laid it in the middle of the Temple. And on the next day, I King Solomon, went into the Temple of God and sat in deep distress about the stone of the end of the corner. And when I entered the Temple, the flask stood up and walked around some seven steps and then fell on its mouth and did homage to me. And I marvelled that even along with the bottle the demon still had power and could walk about; and I commanded it to stand up. And the flask stood up, and stood on its feet all blown out.

And I questioned him, saying: "Tell me, who art thou?" And the spirit within said: "I am the demon called Ephippas, that is in Arabia." And I said to him: "Is this thy name?" And he answered: "Yes; wheresoever I will, I alight and set fire and do to death."

122.

And I said to him: "By what angel art thou frustrated?" And he answered: "By the only-ruling God, that hath authority over me even to be heard. He that is to be born of a virgin and crucified by the Jews on a cross. Whom the angels and archangels worship. He doth frustrate me, and enfeeble me of my great strength, which has been given me by my father the devil." And I said to him: "What canst thou do?" And he answered: "I am able to remove mountains, to overthrow the oaths of kings. I wither trees and make their leaves to fall off." And I said to him: "Canst thou raise this stone, and lay it for the beginning of this corner which exists in the fair plan of the Temple?" And he said: "Not only raise this, O king; but also, with the help of the demon who presides over the Red Sea, I will bring up the pillar of air, and will stand it where thou wilt in Jerusalem."

123.

Saying this, I laid stress on him, and the flask became as if depleted of air. And I placed it under the stone, and (the spirit) girded himself up, and lifted it up top of the flask. And the flask went up the steps, carrying the stone, and laid it down at the end of the entrance of the Temple. And I Solomon, beholding the stone raised aloft and placed on a foundation, said: "Truly the Scripture is fulfilled, which says: 'The stone which the builders rejected on trial, that same is become the head of the corner.' For this it is not mine to grant, but God's, that the demon should be strong enough to lift up so great a stone and deposit it in the place I wished."

124.

And Ephippas led the demon of the Red Sea with the column. And they both took the column and raised it aloft from the earth. And I outwitted these two spirits, so that they could not shake the entire earth in a moment of time. And then I sealed round with my ring on this side and that, and said: "Watch." And the spirits have remained upholding it until this day, for proof of the wisdom vouchsafed to me. And there the pillar was hanging of enormous size, in mid air, supported by the winds. And thus the spirits appeared underneath, like air, supporting it. And if one looks fixedly, the pillar is a little oblique, being supported by the spirits; and it is so to day.

125.

And I Solomon questioned the other spirit which came up with the pillar from the depth of the Red Sea. And I said to him: "Who art thou, and what calls thee? And what is thy business? For I hear many things about thee." And the demon answered: "I, O King Solomon, am called Abezithibod. I am a descendant of the archangel. Once as I sat in the first heaven, of which the name is Ameleouth -- I then am a fierce spirit and winged, and with a single wing, plotting against every spirit under heaven. I was present when Moses went in before Pharaoh, king of Egypt, and I hardened his heart. I am he whom Iannes and Iambres invoked homing with Moses in Egypt. I am he who fought against Moses with wonders with signs."

126.

I said therefore to him: "How wast thou found in the Red Sea?" And he answered: "In the exodus of the sons of Israel I hardened the heart of Pharaoh. And I excited his heart and that of his ministers. And I caused them to pursue after the children of Israel. And Pharaoh followed with (me) and all the Egyptians. Then I was present there, and we followed together. And we all came up upon the Red Sea. And it came to pass when the children of Israel had crossed over, the water returned and hid all the host of the Egyptians and all their might. And I remained in the sea, being kept under this pillar. But when Ephippas came, being sent by thee, shut up in the vessel of a flask, he fetched me up to thee."

127.

I, therefore, Solomon, having heard this, glorified God and adjured the demons not to disobey me, but to remain supporting the pillar. And they both sware, saying: "The Lord thy God liveth, we will not let go this pillar until the world's end. But on whatever day this stone fall, then shall be the end of the world."

128.

And I Solomon glorified God, and adorned the Temple of the Lord with all fair-seeming. And I was glad in spirit in my kingdom, and there was peace in my days. And I took wives of my own from every land, who were numberless. And I marched against the Jebusaeans, and there I saw Jebusaean, daughter of a man: and fell violently in love with her, and desired to take her to wife along with my other wives. And I said to their priests: "Give me the Sonmanites (i.e. Shunammite) to wife." But the priests of Moloch said to me: "If thou lovest this maiden, go in and worship our gods, the great god Raphan and the god called Moloch." I therefore was in fear of the glory of God, and did not follow to worship. And I said to them: "I will not worship a strange god. What is this proposal, that ye compel me to do so much?" But they said: "... by our fathers."

129.

And when I answered that I would on no account worship strange gods, they told the maiden not to sleep with me until I complied and sacrificed to the gods. I then was moved, but crafty Eros brought and laid by her for me five grasshoppers, saying: "Take these grasshoppers, and crush them together in the name of the god Moloch; and then will I sleep with you." And this I actually did. And at once the Spirit of God departed from me, and I became weak as well as foolish in my words. And after that I was obliged by her to build a temple of idols to Baal, and to Rapha, and to Moloch, and to the other idols.

130.

I then, wretch that I am, followed her advice, and the glory of God quite departed from me; and my spirit was darkened, and I became the sport of idols and demons. Wherefore I wrote out this Testament, that ye who get possession of it may pity, and attend to the last things, and not to the first. So that ye may find grace for ever and ever. Amen.

PS *ost* **S** *criptum*

Conybeare was far from being a dry scholar…

About F. C. Conybeare

Pseudepigrapha

VAMzzz Publishing

1

Frederick Cornwallis Conybeare

Biography Conybeare

Frederick Cornwallis Conybeare
(14 September 1856 – 9 January 1924)
was a British orientalist, Fellow of
University College, Oxford, and Professor
of Theology at the University of Oxford.
He was the third son of a barrister, John
Charles Conybeare, and grandson of the
geologist William Daniel Conybeare.

Conybeare pioneered Armenian scholarship
in England. He was educated at Tonbridge
School and University College, Oxford,
where he obtained a double first in classical
languages, philosophy and ancient history. He
was then elected a fellow of the college; but,
benefitting from a private income, and finding
the round of college business somewhat
unchallenging, he resigned, and on the advice
of the great orientalist D.S. Margoliouth,
devoted himself to the Armenian language.
Later he took up Georgian too.

Conybeare was far from being a dry scholar.
He expressed his opinions on matters
touching beyond the sphere of scholarship
with a passion unusual in a linguistic
specialist of his time. His first venture into
controversy was to give a strong support
to Alfred Dreyfus against the anti-Semitic
French establishment. This resulted in his
book *The Dreyfus Case* in 1889. ▶

▶ Secondly, his study of Christian origins made him a religious sceptic.

One of his best-known works is *Myth, Magic, and Morals* (1909), later reissued under the title *The Origins of Christianity*. This has been read both as strong criticism of the Jesus myth theory, making Conybeare a supporter of the historical Jesus; but also as an attack on aspects of orthodox Christianity itself. The book is now placed alongside Frazer's *The Golden Bough* and Freud's *Totem and Taboo*.

The third deed of dissent was giving him more trouble than the first two. In 1914 Conybeare declared that H. H. Asquith and Sir Edward Grey were mainly responsible for the outbreak of the first world war. This made him very unpopular in Oxford, and in 1917 he left north Oxford to live in Folkstone for the rest of his life.

He was married to Mary Emily. In 1924 Conybeare died, aged 68, and was buried in Brompton Cemetery, London. ■

Other publications:

- *Outlines of a Philosophy of Religion by Hermann Lotze translator (1892)*
- *The Armenian Apology and Acts of Apollonius, and Other Monuments of Early Christianity (1894)*
- *The Demonology of the New Testament I (1896)*
- *About the Contemplative Life; or the Fourth Book of the Treatise Concerning Virtues, by Philo Judaeus editor (1895)*
- *The Dreyfus Case (1898)*
- *The Key of Truth, a Manual of the Paulician Church of Armenia (1898)*
- *The Story of Ahikar from the Syriac, Arabic, Armenian, Ethiopic, Greek and Slavonic Versions with J. Rendel Harris and Agnes Smith Lewis (1898)*
- *Rituale Armenorum Being the Administration of the Sacraments & the Breviary Rites of the Armenian Church Together with the Greek Rites of Baptism & Epiphany edited from the oldest manuscripts with Arthur John Maclean (1905)*
- *Selections from the Septuagint According to the Text of Swete with St. George Stock, later as A Grammar of Septuagint Greek online (1905)*
- *The Armenian version of Revelation, Apocalypse of John the Divine editor (1907)*
- *Myth, Magic, and Morals: A Study of Christian Origins (1909)*

'His study of Christian origins made him a religious sceptic.'

- *History of New Testament Criticism (1910)*
- *The Ring of Pope Xystus, Together with the Prologue of Rufinus (1910)*
- *The Life of Apollonius of Tyana: The Epistles of Apollonius and the Treatise of Eusebius. Philostratus translator, Loeb Classical Library, two volumes (1912)*
- *A Catalogue of the Armenian Manuscripts in the British Museum (1913)*
- *The Historical Christ; or, An investigation of the views of Mr. J. M. Robertson, Dr. A. Drews, and Prof. W. B. Smith (1914)*
- *Russian Dissenters (1921)*
- *The Armenian Church: Heritage and Identity. (St. Vartan Press: New York, 2001) edited by the Rev. Nerses Vrej Nersessian*
- *The Eusebian Form of the Text of Matthew 28:19*

Apocrypha and Pseudepigrapha

The Testament of Solomon belongs to a series of Jewish writings from the Second Temple Period on biblical items and/or figures which were excluded from the Hebrew Bibel (Tanakh, Tenach); these writings are known as the Apocrypha and Pseudepigrapha.

The Apocrypha ("hidden books") are Jewish books from that period not preserved in the Tanakh, but included in the Latin (Vulgate) and Greek (Septuagint) Old Testaments. The Apocrypha are still regarded as part of the canon of the Roman Catholic and Orthodox churches, and as such, their number is fixed.

Pseudepigrapha ("falsely attributed") are Jewish scriptures of the same period, which were attributed to authors who did not actually write them. The Pseudepigrapha were written by pagan authors, and names drawn from the repertoire of biblical personalities, such as Adam, Noah, Enoch, etcetera. The Pseudepigrapha were not included in the Bible, Apocrypha, or rabbinic literature, and although they resemble the Apocrypha, Christian opinion leaders did and do not regard them as God inspired books.

The best known Pseudepigraphic work is the *Book of Enoch*. This is also the oldest of all Jewish works not included in the Bible. ▶

▶ It was written in the third or the late fourth century BC. The oldest copies of the *Book of Enoch* were discovered among the Dead Sea Scrolls.

The latest of the Apocrypha and Pseudepigrapha are the Apocalypses of Ezra and Baruch, written in 70 CE. Some of the apocryphal works were known in Jewish tradition throughout the Middle Ages, not necessarily in their full texts, but in shortened and retold versions. Thus, versions of the *Books of Judith, Ben Sira, Maccabees* and parts of *Wisdom of Solomon* were familiar to Jewish scholars. However, these works never achieved wide acceptance in Judaism and remained curiosities.

Fragment of 1 Enoch

Select list of Pseudepigrapha

- Apocalypse of Abraham
- The First Book of Adam and Eve
- The Second Book of Adam and Eve
- Apocalypse of Adam
- Syriac Apocalypse of Baruch.
- Biblical Antiquities or Pseudo-Philo
- Book of Enoch
- Book of the Secrets of Enoch – also known as Enoch II or the Slavonic Enoch
- Books of Giants
- Fourth Book of Ezra
- Book of Jubilees
- Lives of the Prophets
- Testament of Moses or Assumption of Moses
- Testament of Solomon
- The Psalms of Solomon
- The Odes of Solomon
- The Letter of Aristeas
- Fourth Book of Maccabees
- The Story of Ahikar
- Testament of Reuben
- Testament of Simeon
- Testament of Levi
- The Testament of Judah
- The Testament of Issachar
- The Testament of Zebulun
- The Testament of Dan
- The Testament of Naphtali
- The Testament Of Gad
- The Testament of Asher
- The Testament of Joseph
- The Testament of Benjamin
- The Sibylline Oracles

VAMzzz Publishing

Paper books

VAMzzz Publishing is located in the very centre of old Amsterdam, in The Netherlands. Our publishing company creates high quality revised editions of five star occult, witchcraft, Gothic and esoteric classics, mostly written in the Fin de siècle-period and early 20th century.

As a publisher, we deeply respect the writer of any book we choose, so we join our forces (top level graphic design & thirty years of occult studies) to produce enchanting volumes which maximize the reading pleasure and inform, often with extra added information. In contrast to the current trend of digital screen addiction, we think, this variety of literature needs to be presented on paper. *No e-books, but real books!*

Apart from republications of valuable but forgotten books, we are also in the preparation of new publications on topics such as self-healing, magic, new astrology and more.

Previews of all books including a complete table of contents can be viewed on www.vamzzz.com. More books will be added to the list. *VAMzzz Publishing* strives to publish new volumes every month. Please visit our website regularly for the latest updates.

VAMzzz Publishing
P.O. Box 3340
1001 AC Amsterdam
The Netherlands
contactvamzzz@gmail.com
www.vamzzz.com

Amazons - Two publications in one book -
I. *The Amazons* by Guy Cadogan Rothery
II. *Religious Cults Associated With the Amazons*
   by Florence Mary Bennett
328 pages, Paperback, ISBN 9789492355089

Contents I: The Amazons of Antiquity – Amazons
in Far Asia – Modern Amazons of the Caucasus –
Amazons of Europe – Amazons of Africa – Amazons of
America – The Amazon Stones.
Contents II: The Amazons in Greek legend – The Great
Mother – Ephesian Artemis – Artemis Astrateia and
Apollo Amazonius – Ares.

Ophiolatreia
Rites and Mysteries of Serpent Worship
Author: Hargrave Jennings
186 pages, Paperback, ISBN 9789492355126

An account of the rites and mysteries connected with
the origin, rise and development of serpent worship in
various parts of the world, enriched with interesting
traditions, and a full description of the celebrated
serpent mounds & temples, the whole forming an
exposition of one of the phases of phallic, or sex
worship.

Voodoos and Obeahs
Phases of West India Witchcraft
by Joseph J. Williams
374 pages, Paperback, ISBN 9789492355119

This work goes into great depth concerning the New
World-African connection and is highly recommended if
you want a deep understanding of the dramatic historical
background of Haitian and Jamaican magic and witchcraft,
and the profound influence of imperialism, slavery and
racism on its development. Williams includes numerous
quotations from rare documents and books on the topic.

Taboo, Magic, Spirits
A study of primitive elements in Roman religion
by Eli Edward Burriss
200 pages, Paperback, ISBN 9789492355034

In Ancient Rome Mana was the term used for a mysterious, magical medium, which could be helpful or harmful (Taboo). Just like the Chinese qi, it could empower the positive and the negative. Contents: Mana, Magic and Animism – Positive and Negative Mana (Taboo) – Miscellaneous Taboos – Magic Acts: The General Principles – Removing Evils by - Magic Acts – Incantation and Prayer– Naturalism and Animism.

Chaldean Magic
It's Origin and Development
by François Lenormant
454 pages, Paperback, ISBN 9789492355027

The essentials of magic in Chaldea are presented inside a context of comparison or contrast to Egyptian, Median, Turanian, Finno-Tartarian and Akkadian magic, mythologies, religion and speech. Interesting is the Chaldean demonology, with its incubus, succubus, vampire, nightmare and many Elemental spirits, most of them coalesced with the primal powers of nature.

Unicorn
A mythological investigation
by Robert Brown Jr.
124 pages, Paperback, ISBN 9789492355072

Brown Jr. believes the unicorn to be a lunar symbol, and draws on mythology from a wide range of sources all over the world to build his case. The author discusses the heraldic use of the unicorn, relates the creature to ancient goddesses like Astarte, Hecate en the Gorgon Medusa, and provides the reader with lost esoteric Moon-lore.

Là-Bas
A Journey into the Self
by Joris-Karl Huysmans
378 pages, Paperback, ISBN 9789492355058

The plot of *Là-Bas* concerns the novelist Durtal, who is disgusted by the emptiness and vulgarity of the modern world. He seeks relief by turning to the study of the Middle Ages. Through his contacts in Paris, Durtal discovers that Satanism is not a thing of the past but alive and kicking in turn of the century France. The novel culminates with a description of a black mass.

Devil-worship in France
Or The Question of Lucifer
by Arthur Edward Waite
240 pages, Paperback, ISBN 9789492355065

In *Devil-Worship in France,* Waite attempts to discern what is genuine from what is fake in the evidence of 19th century Satanism. To get the answers he spends a great deal of time investigating the French Masonic echelon, debunking a "conspiracy of falsehood" and determining what should be understood by Satanism and what not. Huysmans' diabolical novel *Là-Bas* (1891) inspired Waite to write this sceptical analysis.

Aradia
Gospel of the Witches
by Charles Godfrey Leland
174 pages, Paperback, ISBN 9789492355010

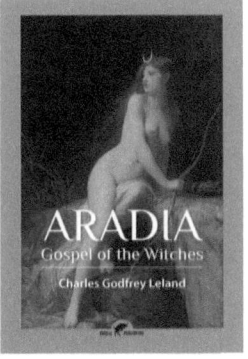

This wonderful book describes the creation according to Italian witch-lore. We also read about the witch-meeting or sabbath (treguenda) and the book contains many original magical recipes, like spells for love and good fortune. Diana is further connected to the Moon and the fairy world.

Fairy Mythology *(Volume 1)*
Romance and Superstition of Various Countries 1
by Thomas Keightley
404 pages, Paperback, ISBN 9789492355096

Fairy Mythology *(Volume 2)*
Romance and Superstition of Various Countries 2
by Thomas Keightley
404 pages, Paperback, ISBN 9789492355102

The term Fairy covers all kinds of nature spirits, not just the tiny sugar sweet creatures hovering around flowers. A unique and impressive book on this subject, published in a revised 2 volume-edition. No wiccan or pagan can afford to leave these books unopened. About Elves, Dwarfs, Kobolds, Trolls, Changelings, Meremaids, Nisses, Fairies, Brownies, Puck and other Elemental spirits all over the world.

Etruscan Magic & Occult Remedies
(Two volumes in one book)
Charles Godfrey Leland
628 pages, Paperback, ISBN 9789492355003

Part One of the book offers complete and detailed insight in the Etruscan and Roman rooted pantheon of the Tuscan Streghe (witches). Part Two describes many of their spells, incantations, sorcery and several lost divination methods. Much information in this book, Leland received first hand from the Tuscan witches Maddalena and Marietta.